Monday Morni[ng]

Start your week right.... All year long!

By

Yetty Iriah

Jenny,
You are a blessed woman.
Never forget that!
Yetty 24/4/19

Copyright © 2019 by Yetty Iriah

Scripture quotations are taken from The Holy Bible, New King James Version®. Copyright © 1982 by Thomas Nelson. Used by permission. All rights reserved.

Scripture quotations are taken from The Holy Bible, New International Version® NIV® Copyright © 1973 1978 1984 2011 by Biblica, Inc. Used by permission. All rights reserved worldwide.

Scripture quotations are taken from the *Holy Bible*, New Living Translation, copyright © 1996, 2004, 2015 by Tyndale House Foundation. Used by permission of Tyndale House Publishers, Inc., Carol Stream, Illinois 60188.

All rights reserved. ISBN: 978-0-244-52165-3

No part of this book may be reproduced in any form or by any electronic or mechanical means, including information storage and retrieval systems, without written permission from the author, except for the use of brief quotations in a book review.

DEDICATION

This book is dedicated to an amazing group of women;
my DWJ- Dinner with Jesus sisters.
You joined the boat when we didn't even have a destination!
It has been an absolute honour to have served the Lord with you for the last ten years!
Together we will continue to change lives.
.... One at a time!

God Bless You!

ABOUT MONDAY MORNING COFFEE

'Monday Morning Coffee' is a compendium of God-inspired light-hearted weekly reflective messages to start off your busy week all year long!

I started the Monday Morning Coffee blog in November 2015 during an extremely challenging period in my life. I would prefer to say that I stumbled into it as I was journaling one early Monday morning, and out of the blue the name 'Monday Morning Coffee' jumped out at me!

It has been an absolute pleasure to serve my steaming hot cups of 'Monday Morning Coffee' to friends like you all over the world each week for the last 4 years via my blog and on social media platforms.

This year I was inspired to turn my blog into a weekly devotional.

.... This is it!

ACKNOWLEDGMENTS

This "book-baby" was midwifed by so many wonderful people but it will be absolutely impossible to name them all!

First, I give all the glory to God who has inspired me to share His heart every Monday without fail for the last 4 years and gave me several opportunities to write this book. Thank you for guiding my trembling steps and for reminding me that victory is inevitable in You! .... I made it in the end!

To Paul, my husband, best friend and sounding board, thanks for your love and patience throughout this journey and particularly for spurring me on to fulfil my God-given purpose.

To my children Juny, Tobias, Emmanuella and Daniella; the four jewels in my crown, you are my reward from God. Together we have grown to become who we are in Christ. You are destined for the top; the seeds of greatness have been sown in you.

To my accountability partner and chief midwife Bukky Ayoade, you saw the vision of this book from day one and believed in me when I was at my lowest ebb, and kept pushing me until it became a reality. Your dreams will come true too.

To my pastors Tim and Helen Roberts, thank you for giving me the room to fly and fulfil purpose unhindered.

To all my friends and family your encouragement over the last 4 years kept me going. Your support on the Monday Morning Coffee Blog and on social media platforms every Monday are the reason I awake each Monday morning inspired to impact at least one more life. Thank you for all the joy you brought to this wonderful adventure. The Lord will beautify your lives too.

To all the ladies at the Monday Coffee Morning meetings who use my write-ups, I thank you for making it worthwhile.

To all the lovely people who will buy, read and share this book, thank you for the privilege to be part of your busy lives each week. As you read, may the Lord will show up in your lives in unexplainable ways.

.

....There's nothing like a hot steaming cup of Monday Morning Coffee!

WHAT OTHERS ARE SAYING ABOUT MONDAY MORNING COFFEE

"Yetty is an inspiration - her wit and insight, and most of all her love for God and the wisdom she brings to everyday life, brings the Bible to life in this book and will brighten your day!"
- Rev Tim Roberts, Senior Leader, Wellspring Church Watford, UK

"I am always amazed at Yetty's unique way of writing. She has a way with words and imagery that keeps one longing for and looking for the next write-up. I am pleased that Yetty has now compiled all those wisdom nuggets into a book."
-Bola Ogedengbe. Pastor, Kingdom Arena, Luton UK

"Yetty's Monday Morning Coffee blogs have been such an inspiration and I am encouraged just by reading... The words speak directly to me!"
-Essie Duncan. Accra, Ghana

"Yetty's write-ups have been very helpful in giving me focus at the start of each week, and help keep my mind on spiritual things."
-Angela Ajise. Sacramento, California, Usa

"We have used the Monday Morning Coffee messages for our Monday Coffee Morning meetings at church and have found them to be very encouraging and people have been keen to attend to hear the message and reflect on the bible passages associated with the Monday Morning Coffee blog. ....Truly inspiring."
-Caroline martins. uk

"I have had the pleasure of reading Monday Morning Coffee over the last 2 years, as a silent partaker. I have found it to be very insightful, inspirational and profound."
-Dr 'Koye Adenuga- Ann Arbor, Michigan USA

"I've enjoyed reading Yetty's God-inspired messages, sent on Mondays (never failing). They usually focus on one theme and manage to convey a very thoughtful message in just a few words. I admire how she can cover such a wide variety of topics. Thank you Yetty for providing words of inspiration for our busy weeks!"
-Kevin Obi- UK

"Monday Morning Coffee has truly been a weekly succinct reminder of life wonderful blessings. It energises me to press on in my life's journey even during the difficult times. Thank you Yetty for heeding God's call upon your life. May the Lord continue to use you for the advancement of his kingdom and of destinies."
-Elizabeth Osifo. Hemel Hempstead, UK

"Monday Morning Coffee is always 'served' hot because I read it immediately after my morning exercise, (adrenaline still pumping). It touches on reality, our triumphs, struggles, and day to day living. Monday Morning Coffee is truly Holy Spirit-inspired. I pray the Lord will use it to touch lives through Yetty."
-Mary Dodiyi-Manuel-Abuja, Nigeria

"Like coffee, Monday Morning Coffee has been to me a stimulant, a pick-me-up to start my work week. It's brief, easy to read, and easy to support with scripture. It causes me to reflect and occasionally recognise my areas of struggle followed by a commitment to work on them. Monday Morning Coffee!...Recommended for all coffee lovers and those who love them!"
-Modupe Afolabi- Lagos Nigeria

"Monday morning coffee came to me at the exact point of my need when I required some lifting up. It was really a case of the Lord working in mysterious ways as the words spoke specifically and directly to me. Since then I have looked forward to them at the start of each week and they continue to inspire and encourage me."
- Dr Odu Adu. UK

"I have been doing a lot of travelling and just caught up with all the Monday Morning Coffees so I am caffeine-full. Yetty's style of writing is such a blessing; short and punchy. One of my favourites is the 'clogged drains'. Forgiveness is for our own benefit really".
Dr Tosin Talabi-Royal Air Force, Lincolnshire, UK

"As my big sister, Yetty has always been an inspiration, and when she started her Monday Morning Coffee blog four years ago, I was just blown away by her degree of consistency and attention to detail. This book is a keeper!"
-Chizoro Williams-Middlesex, UK

"Monday Coffee is inspirational, encouraging, edifying, and empowering, it allows one to reflect on life's issues, admonishes, and keeps one on the straight and narrow. A real blessing!
- Helen Boadi. Watford UK

"Monday Morning Coffee has been a great blessing to me. Sometimes when I am at a crossroad, Yetty talks on a subject that speaks to me directly. It has been a real blessing to read, and I look forward to it every Monday"
- Helen Oghenekaro. Lagos, Nigeria

"Monday Morning Coffee allows me to reflect on the everyday realities of life. The words strengthen me in areas where I have been lacking or taken for granted. Most importantly I am reminded that I am not only unique, but that there's a reason and purpose for my existence, which I must fulfil."
'Deola Salako, Hemel Hempstead, UK

"Yetty's Monday Morning Coffee blogs have been a source of inspiration to me. Her simple analogies drive home the essence of our Christian faith and values, capture the Spirit-led life, and provoke one to godliness. I pray that God continually enriches Yetty's knowledge and understanding of His word for the benefit of her readers."
- Toby Iweka. Pastor, Evangelist, Josea ministries

"I am an avid reader of Yetty's Monday Morning Coffee columns which over time have become an integral part of my starter-pack for the week. Always just about the right length, the Monday Morning Coffee columns are inspiring, insightful and thought- provoking definitely an uplifting experience for any reader regardless of the day of the week they are read."
- Tee Mann- Legal Practitioner UK

"Monday Morning Coffee is a guided masterpiece. Yetty's words bring great meaning to the grey areas of our lives. The impact her write-ups have had on my life has been mind-blowing."
-Marylene Isaiah -UK

FOREWORD 1

What a privilege it is for me to write about this book, and especially about Yetty as the author. I met Yetty in a meeting once, and since then I have been invited to speak at the annual conferences that she hosts. It's been such an honour for me working alongside this great woman whose heart burns to help people to pursue their dreams and see them find happiness and fulfilment.

Transforming "Monday Morning Coffee" into a book is a phenomenal idea considering how deep these seeds have been sown in people's hearts. The thoughts and challenging words that Yetty shares through WhatsApp on Mondays, actually makes all the difference in people's lives, to the point where she has built an audience throughout the internet in such a way that these people don't hesitate to attend the conferences she hosts within the year.

One of Yetty's biggest traits is her passion for people, a heart burning for them to be restored from their weaknesses, guiding them into a new platform of life, and leading them to experience God at a very high level, as the Author and consumer of our faith.

Monday Morning Coffee is not just any other book, but it is a Legacy Builder, a book that will help you with just a few simple words, deal with situations that come to destabilise your life.

I highly recommend this book for your meditation. I am totally convinced that through it you will find peace and happiness.

PASTOR EDDIE NUNES
SUNRISE CHURCH, HEMEL HEMPSTEAD UK

FOREWORD 2

I am grateful to God for inspiring Yetty to write 'Monday Morning Coffee'. It is uplifting, encouraging and inspirational.

When you think on a Monday you are starting a new week with challenges ahead, 'Monday Morning Coffee' is a welcomed warmth to the spirit and the soul. You imagine yourself drinking words of wisdom and encouragement to warm your spirit and awaken your soul ready for the week ahead.

God has many ways of speaking to us, this is one of them. I highly recommend this book and pray that God will bless you as you start your day with words of wisdom.

PASTOR LADE AJUMOBI
FOUNDER, PRAYING PARENTS INTERNATIONAL

CONTENTS

About Monday Morning Coffee
Acknowledgments
What Others Are Saying About Monday Morning Coffee
Foreword 1
Foreword 2
Week 1-Begin Again!
Week 2- Risk Worth Taking
Week 3- What Time is it?
Week 4- Return to Joy!
Week 5- Climb Your Sycamore Tree
Week 6- The Wake-Up Call
Week 7- The Odd Man Out
Week 8- Selective Memory
Week 9- Messed Up?
Week 10-Nothing to Hide
Week 11- Approval Addiction
Week 12- A Fighting Chance!
Week 13-What's Your Plan B?
Week 14- The Furnace Club
Week 15- Just in Time!
Week 16- Limbo Valley
Week 17- The Finisher!
Week 18- No Free Benefits!
Week 19- Name Your Hurricane!
Week 20- Small is Enough!
Week 21- Distinctly Unique
Week 22-Shoes Off!.... Please!
Week 23- Busy Bees!
Week 24- Who Needs a Monument?
Week 25- All That Drama!
Week 26- This is War!

Week 27- Let's Go!
Week 28- A Sudden Breakthrough!
Week 29- Shhh!.....Zip it!
Week 30- Hard Pressed?
Week 31- The Masters Business
Week 32- I Can See You!
Week 33- Which Door Lord?
Week 34- Build!
Week 35- Enjoy the Scenery
Week 36- Hush!....Hush!
Week 37- Rejects Wanted!
Week 38- Rain! Rain!....Go Away!
Week 39- The Chain-breaker!
Week 40- Which is your Cross?
Week 41- Attention!....Fruit Lovers
Week 42- The Empty Waiting Room
Week 43- Call the Doctor!
Week 44- Divided Loyalty
Week 45- The Hall of Fame
Week 46- For the Fashionista
Week 47- ....That Smells so Good!
Week 48- The Dream Team
Week 49- The Soil of Uncertainty
Week 50- Faith on a Tightrope
Week 51- Bring Your Gifts
Week 52- New Life!...Here I come!
Your Bonus Cup of Coffee!....Sing a New Song!
Book Review
Thank You

Week 1

BEGIN AGAIN!

H appy New Year!

What better way to start this year than with the amazing lyrics of this old song by Jimmy Cliff:

I can see clearly now, the rain is gone,
I can see all obstacles in my way
Gone are the dark clouds that had me blind
It's gonna be a bright (bright), bright (bright) Sun-Shiny day.

I think I can make it now, the pain is gone
All of the bad feelings have disappeared
Here is the rainbow I've been prayin' for
It's gonna be a bright (bright), bright (bright) Sun-Shiny day.

(If you don't know this song then you are probably too young!)

This year I am expectant, and I want you to be as well. I am confident that we shall be leaping from one breakthrough to another! Peace and joy will not cease from our lives and good health and abundance are our portion!

Most importantly I pray that we will serve God with wholehearted devotion this year. Remember, you have been set free! Express yourself and live your dreams!

<u>**Welcome to 2020....Your best year yet!**</u>

PRAYER FOR THE WEEK
Lord I begin again with you today. I don't know what the year will bring but I choose to trust that I am safe and secure in your loving arms.

**Yetty Iriah
Monday Morning Coffee Copyright 2020**
Photo: Pixabay.com

Reflective Notes

What are your goals for the new year?

Just to get through it! feel very low this morning - but will trust in God that He will lift my spirits

What steps will you take to improve your relationship with God this year?

Keep focusing on God not myself

Week 2

A RISK WORTH TAKING

Happy Monday people!

If the Lord is leading you to take a huge leap this year, then this post is for you!

Last year a close friend left a thriving family business she had jointly run with her husband for several years to launch out into something new. Stepping into the unknown was a huge risk, but it paid off and today she is hugely successful and enjoying her new adventure.

At the end of 2015, after almost a year of prayerful deliberation, I also made a bold decision to trust the Lord and walk onto uncharted waters, turning my back on the familiar and comfortable. It was tough, but so many miracles have happened along the way, and the

Lord has surrounded me with wonderful people. Today I am walking in my purpose without regret.

Moving beyond the safe and familiar is essential for growth. If Peter had not stepped out of the boat he would never have known he could walk on water!

Are you ready for some great adventures this year?

Take the risk! ....Miracles await you! ....You too can walk on water!

ACTION FOR THE WEEK
1. What risks are you being led to take this year?
2. What obstacles are stopping you?
3. Prayerfully consider how you will remove these obstacles?
4. Start today.

Yetty Iriah
Monday Morning Coffee Copyright 2020
Photo: Tobi pexels.com

Reflective Notes

What have you learnt today?

What changes will you make this week?

Week 3

WHAT TIME IS IT?

Happy Monday people!

This morning let's reflect on some soul-stirring truths.

Someone once said that the opportunity of a lifetime is one that occurs only in the lifetime of that opportunity. We serve a time-conscious God and must make use of every opportunity He gives us in a timely manner. Some have missed golden opportunities to lead their spouses, friends or terminally ill loved ones to Christ.

When Noah was building the Ark, the people in his town thought he was out of his mind. One day Noah, his family and all the animals walked into the Ark, the door was shut, and the rains came down.... The people had missed the boat. **(Genesis 6:1-22)**

Ten virgins were waiting for the arrival of the bridegroom, the five foolish virgins went to buy more oil for their lamps, and while they were gone the bridegroom arrived. They had missed their chance too. **(Matthew 25:1-13)**

One day the trumpet will sound to herald the arrival of the King of Kings!
....Will you be ready?....The clock is ticking!

PRAYER FOR THE WEEK
Lord, I accept the responsibility for missing the great opportunities you have brought my way. Forgive me for letting you down. Give me a second chance and may I be ready for that great day that dawns closer and closer in Jesus Name.

Yetty Iriah
Monday Morning Coffee Copyright 2020
Photo: Pixabay.com

Reflective Notes

What have you learnt today?

What changes will you make this week?

Week 4

RETURN TO JOY

Happy Monday people!

Is your life under a siege? Did you wake up today wondering how things got this bad? Are you trying to claw your way out of a hole, but sinking even deeper still? Well, my friend you are not alone.

The Syrian army once set up a siege around Samaria. The situation was so dire that camel dung was sold as food and mothers were forced to eat their children! One night God caused the Syrians to hear a strange noise; they panicked and ran for their dear lives, leaving their belongings behind to be plundered by the Israelites. Overnight the Israelites transitioned from abject lack to surplus! God sure has a sense of humour. **(2 Kings 6:24-7:19)**

Breathe!....Joy is coming to your home too!

PRAYER FOR THE WEEK
I decree and declare that every siege over your life is lifted this morning. Behold the Lord; the lifter of the siege and giver of joy reigns in your life! It is well with you.

Yetty Iriah
Monday Morning Coffee Copyright 2020
Photo: Pixabay.com

Reflective Notes

What have you learnt today?
_____
_____
_____
_____
_____
_____
_____
_____
_____
_____

What changes will you make this week?
_____
_____
_____
_____
_____
_____
_____
_____
_____

Week 5

CLIMB YOUR SYCAMORE TREE

Happy Monday people!

What are your plans for the new month? For several years the Lord had been nudging on my heart to start a big project, but I kept putting it off, because all I could just see in front of me were my own limitations and the obstacles that other people had put in my way.

I kept procrastinating until the Lord reminded me of Zaccheus the tax collector, an extremely determined short man who ran ahead of the crowd in his bid to see Jesus when He came into his town. When Zaccheus's height got in the way, he did the next best thing; he climbed up the Sycamore tree. **(Luke 19:1-10)**

Desperation and motivation are two attributes that will propel us in the direction of our dreams. Have you been planning to start a business, write that book, apply for that job or mend that relationship? Put that plan into action now!

Are you as desperate as Zaccheus? ....Then climb your Sycamore tree!

PRAYER FOR THE WEEK

Lord I know you will never give me a vision without a provision. This week open my eyes to see the provision you have made for me and give me the courage to go!

Yetty Iriah
Monday Morning Coffee Copyright 2020
Photo: Bestofgreenscreen Copyright123RF.com

Reflective Notes

What have you learnt today?

What changes will you make this week?

Week 6

THE WAKE-UP CALL

Happy Monday People!

This morning I want us to reflect on the story of the two sleeping prostitutes, in King Solomon's judgement. One prostitute slept so deeply she rolled onto her baby crushing him to death, then swapped him with the baby of the other prostitute who was so deep in sleep too that she did not know when that exchange took place. **(1 Kings 3:16-21)**

....Both mothers were sleeping on duty!

"That night while men slept the enemy came in and planted weeds among the wheat and then he slipped away" (Matthew 13:25)

Today, I sound a clarion call to all parents; the devil is working over-time killing children and exchanging their destinies, just like the babies in this story. Parents arise and return to your prayer altars; we are dealing with a slippery enemy.

This is your wake-up call!
....Open your eyes, it's time to bend those lazy knees!

PRAYER FOR THE WEEK
O Lord, please forgive me for sleeping at my duty post at a time when I should have been watchful. Help me rekindle the fire on my prayer altar and give me the strength to battle for my next generation.

Yetty Iriah
Monday Morning Coffee Copyright 2020
Photo: Pavlo Syvak Copyright 123RF.com

Reflective Notes

What have you learnt today?

What changes will you make this week?

Week 7

THE ODD MAN OUT

Happy Monday people!

Are you one who is easily swayed by popular opinion or do you have a mind of your own?

Under the command of Moses, the children of Israel always moved in the direction of the cloud. If the cloud remained above the tabernacle then they set up camp, and when it lifted it was time to move. They had no control over the timing of the cloud; whether it stayed a year, a month or just a few days. **(Exodus 40:38)**

The same God who led the Israelites then leads us today and His standards are still the same; only this time we are led by the Holy Spirit, and must be prepared to be the lone voice; the one that is often misunderstood, misrepresented and unpopular. Following the crowd is always the easier option for those who crave popularity and like to be celebrated.

We must remember that it was the crowd that shouted, "Crucify Him!" it was the crowd that wanted to stone the woman caught in adultery and it was the crowd that wanted to stone Paul to death.

**<u>If you follow the crowd, you may find yourself in the wrong boat heading in the wrong direction!
....Be wise.</u>**

PRAYER FOR THE WEEK
O Lord, I repent of the times when I have followed the dictates my own heart and listened to popular opinion rather than Your word. Forgive my disobedience.

**Yetty Iriah
Monday Morning Coffee Copyright 2020**
Photo: Elenabsl Copyright 123RF.com

Reflective Notes

What have you learnt today?

What changes will you make this week?

Week 8

SELECTIVE MEMORY?

Happy Monday people!

How good is your memory? Some people have selective memory, so they tend to focus on the negative events and forget the good times. Selective memory often leads to ingratitude.

After their supernatural rescue from Egypt and the miraculous parting of the Red Sea, the children of Israel grumbled at the very first sign of difficulty; they threw a huge tantrum like a dog who lost a bone! They had forgotten so soon; selective memory perhaps. **(Exodus 15: 22-26)**

Very often we also forget what the Lord has done for us; instead we focus on our immediate wants and forget how our needs have been met miraculously all these years. Today most Christians are grumblers, committing the exact same sin that led to the death of thou- sands of Israelites in the wilderness. Grumbling is very contagious, and sadly we are now raising the next generation of grumblers; children with an ultra-sense of entitlement!

<u>**Have you also forgotten so soon?
Today see God's footprints all over your life,
and show some gratitude!**</u>

PRAYER FOR THE WEEK
Lord, forgive me for forgetting so soon the wonders you have performed in my life. Thank you for being faithful though I let you down all the time. This week may I be filled with a spirit of gratitude.

**Yetty Iriah
Monday Morning Coffee Copyright 2020**
Photo: Deskcube Copyright123RF.com

Reflective Notes

What have you learnt today?

What changes will you make this week?

Week 9

MESSED UP?

Happy Monday people!

If you opened your eyes this morning, only to be confronted by the enormity of the mess in your life, then I have great news!

Jesus was no stranger to mess, He came from a lineage of messed up people, lived amongst messed up people in his life time, and died between two messed up people. You are therefore most welcome to this prestigious club!

During His ministry, Jesus encountered individuals who were facing stigmatisation, and those with lives stained with scandal, controversy and contradiction. Jesus did not condemn them but uncovered the greatness in their mess.

"And the earth was without form and void; darkness was upon the face of the deep: and the Spirit of God moved upon the waters." (Genesis 1:2)

The earth also was in a terrible mess until God stepped in, so if your situation is going to change, you will have to let God in too.

There is nothing normal about greatness ....It often a starts with a mess!

PRAYER FOR THE WEEK
O Lord, please reach down from heaven this week and change my messy story, give me a song of praise.

Yetty Iriah
Monday Morning Coffee Copyright 2020
Photo: Pixabay.com

Reflective Notes

What have you learnt today?
_____
_____
_____
_____
_____
_____
_____
_____
_____
_____

What changes will you make this week?
_____
_____
_____
_____
_____
_____
_____
_____
_____
_____

Week 10

NOTHING TO HIDE

Happy Monday People!

For my last birthday, I was treated to a photoshoot with complimentary hair and makeup. I am always amazed by the talent of modern makeup artists; so skilled at covering any facial imperfection, that one ends up with a brand new face!

I have freckles on both cheeks, but thankfully I am able to cover them successfully with my concealer. People say I have such a flawless face ....I wish! Women, the same goes for our wigs, fake nails, fake eyelashes and fake everything else. Men also have fake hair and vests that give them a semblance of a six- pack! ....It's all a cover-up.

"Come let's settle this," says the LORD. "Though your sins be like scarlet, I will make them white as snow. Though they are red like crimson, I will make them as wool. (Isaiah 1:18)

The Blood of Jesus does not cover up, it cleanses completely! God knows the number of hairs on our head (or wigs!) We serve a God to whom nothing is hidden.

....What are you trying to hide?

PRAYER FOR THE WEEK
Lord heal me of physical and emotional insecurities and help me believe that I am complete in you.

Yetty Iriah
Monday Morning Coffee Copyright 2020
Photo: Dolgachov Copyright 123RF.com

Reflective Notes

What have you learnt today?

What changes will you make this week?

Week 11

APPROVAL ADDICTION

Happy Monday good people!

Are you a people pleaser? Perhaps as a leader in your organisation you hold off from making certain decisions for fear that you could become unpopular. Do you struggle to say "No" to others even when it hurts you? If this is your case, then you may have an approval addiction.

Approval addiction makes you a slave. You can never do enough for others, and the more you do the more they expect from you. Just like all other addictions, approval addiction puts you into bondage from which you will struggle to free yourself; it traps you.

The sad thing about approval addiction is that as Christians we often find ourselves in a dilemma between pleasing God and pleasing man and in all honesty most of the time, we end up pleasing man to our own detriment!

*"I'm not trying to win the approval of men, but of God. If pleasing men were my goal,
I would not be Christ's servant." (Galatians 1:10)*

The reality is that not everyone will agree with our views or opinions.

If saying "Yes" will hurt God....Just say "No"!

PRAYER FOR THE WEEK
Lord, forgive me for pleasing others rather than You. May I do your will and believe that I am already approved by you.

Yetty Iriah
Monday Morning Coffee Copyright 2020
Photo: Raywoo Copyright 123RF.com

Reflective Notes

What have you learnt today?
_____
_____
_____
_____
_____
_____
_____
_____
_____
_____

What changes will you make this week?
_____
_____
_____
_____
_____
_____
_____
_____
_____
_____

Week 12

A FIGHTING CHANCE!

Happy Monday people!

I once listened to foremost Ghanaian preacher Archbishop Nicolas Duncan-Williams tell a story about his early life. He was born to a single mother, and as a young boy he was a terror in his neighbourhood and written off by his family. Things were so bad that at one point his mother wished he were dead, but the Lord had a higher purpose in mind, and He raised up an army of praying women. Today the Archbishop is touching lives all over the world.

Good things often come in damaged packages. We can all remember some of our childhood friends who were also written off, and today we can testify to the great men and women most have now become.

"There is hope for your future," says the Lord ....Your children shall return to their own land"
(Jeremiah 31:17)

Don't give up! The battle for that difficult child will be won on your knees. The devil is an evil strategist and he will put what you hate inside what you love, so you give up and stop fighting for what you love!

<u>Don't hang up those boxing gloves yet!</u>
<u>.... Every child deserves a fighting chance</u>!

PRAYER FOR THE WEEK
Lord, please forgive me for giving up on (insert the name/names). I promise not to stop praying until I see Your wonders at work in their life.

Yetty Iriah
Monday Morning Coffee Copyright 2020
Photo: Pixabay.com

Reflective Notes

What have you learnt today?
_____
_____
_____
_____
_____
_____
_____
_____
_____
_____

What changes will you make this week?
_____
_____
_____
_____
_____
_____
_____
_____
_____
_____

Week 13

WHAT'S YOUR PLAN B?

Happy Monday people!

When we say we trust God, do we trust Him explicitly, or do we have other options.... Just in case?

The evening before my son was due to start a new job, he received an email from the company notifying him that he could not start because they had been unable to contact one of his referees. My son spent the whole night trying to contact this referee by phone, email, text, and on all social media platforms without success. This very important referee seemed to have just vanished into thin air.

I knew this was an attack from Hell, so my son and I woke early the next morning to call on God in prayer. It was a 'do or die' situation; we had no Plan B. The answer was instant! By midday this referee just on a whim after several months, decided to check his LinkedIn account and the rest is history!

> "It is impossible to please God without faith. Anyone who comes to Him must believe that God exists and rewards those who sincerely seek him". (Hebrews 11:6)

When Elijah called upon God from Mount Carmel, he had no Plan B, and God showed up! If we have a Plan B, then that is doubt and not faith.

.....Faith has no Plan B!

PRAYER FOR THE WEEK
Lord, today I repent for coming to You with an alternative plan of action; strengthen my faith in Your Word, even when what I see is contrary to what it says.

Yetty Iriah
Monday Morning Coffee Copyright 2020
Photo: Brian Jackson Copyright 123RF.com

Reflective Notes

What have you learnt today?
_____
_____
_____
_____
_____
_____
_____
_____
_____
_____

What changes will you make this week?
_____
_____
_____
_____
_____
_____
_____
_____
_____
_____

Week 14

THE FURNACE CLUB

Happy Monday people!

How are you rolling with the punches that life has thrown you?

I was once privileged to listen to a certain gentleman recounted how difficult life had been for him in the last couple of years. This man had been duped of a large sum of money, he lost his business, his home and almost lost his family and of course by this time all his friends had deserted him.

Remarkably the man said these had been the best years of his life, because he had come to know God so intimately, and he wouldn't have traded them for anything. Without a doubt this man just like the three Hebrew boys had qualified to be a privileged member of The Furnace Club!

"Then the high officers, governors, and advisers saw that the fire had not touched them. Not a hair on their heads was singed, and their clothing was not scorched. They didn't even smell of smoke!"
(Daniel 3:27)

God will never take us around the furnace but will lead us right through it to the other side.

....Always look out for fourth man in the furnace!

PRAYER FOR THE WEEK
As I pass through my difficult seasons, Lord help me hold on to the truth that you will never give me more than I can bear.

Yetty Iriah
Monday Morning Coffee Copyright 2020
Photo: Andre Bortnikov Copyright123RF.com

Reflective Notes

What have you learnt today?

What changes will you make this week?

Week 15

JUST IN TIME!

Happy Monday people!

Easter is here again and this week our focus is on the cross and the painful death Christ endured for our sakes.

No Easter story is more poignant than that of the lucky robber who recognised his need for mercy and cried out to Jesus as he hung next to Him on the cross. It is funny to imagine this robber being one of the first to make it through the pearly gates of Heaven! God sure has a sense of humour. **(Luke23:39-41)**

I can only imagine the shock on the faces of the victims of his reign of terror when they see him in his mansion in Heaven....If they make it!

"For the last shall be first, and the first shall be last......"(Matthew 20:16)

Some people believe they hold exclusive rights to Heaven; the self-righteous, like those who surrounded the woman caught in adultery, armed with their stones of accusation and were shocked that Jesus could forgive her!

<u>Everyone has a chance at the cross!....There's always room for one more!</u>

PRAYER FOR THE WEEK
I am so grateful that you did not change your mind at Calvary Lord! I will never know the debt you paid to set me free. Thank you Lord.

Yetty Iriah
Monday Morning Coffee Copyright 2020
Photo:Udra Copyright123RF.com

Reflective Notes

What have you learnt today?

_____
_____
_____
_____
_____
_____
_____
_____
_____
_____

What changes will you make this week?

_____
_____
_____
_____
_____
_____
_____
_____
_____
_____

Week 16

LIMBO VALLEY

Happy Monday people!

As you sip your hot coffee this morning please spare a kind thought for the plight of millions of refugees in camps all over the world, fleeing war, famine or persecution. How does one hold onto hope when the situation is so realistically hopeless? Sadly, sometimes hope is all we have.

When I watch the news, I cannot help thinking about how it must feel to be uprooted from ones homeland and livelihood, to face an uncertain future. These are families living in 'Limbo Valley'. How does a mother tell her children they may never go back home? How does a father explain to his son that his dream of becoming a doctor may never be realised? Even as I struggle to see how God will permit such devastation, I am reminded that God always has a bigger plan.

The Israelites were in bondage in Egypt for 430 years; they were in their own 'Limbo Valley'. This was the longest layover in history! However, this was just a small part of God's grand masterplan!

<u>Are you living in 'Limbo Valley' too? Ask God to show you a glimpse of His bigger plan.</u>
<u>Grab a chair!....It may just be a long wait too!</u>

PRAYER FOR THE WEEK
Lord, when I consider the areas in my life that are in limbo right now, hope in Your unfailing Word is all I have. Help me trust you for my promised future.

Yetty Iriah
Monday Morning Coffee Copyright 2020
Photo: Fredricofoto Copyright 123RF.com

Reflective Notes

What have you learnt today?

What changes will you make this week?

Week 17

THE FINISHER!

Happy Monday people!

The most compelling story of the 2016 Olympic games was the one about 41-year-old Kuniaki Takizaki, the Japanese- Cambodian athlete who came second to the last in the men's marathon.

The joy on Kuniaki's face as he crossed the finish line brought tears to all eyes as the crowd ecstatically cheered him on. There was no medal for Kuniaki, but he was celebrating because he was a finisher! He had run the race of his life and finished it! The important thing was that He made it across the line!

On the scoreboard there were several names with the letters DNF - (Did Not Finish) next to them; these were the athletes who started but did not finish!

"I have fought the good fight, I have finished the race, I have kept the faith. Now there is in store for me the crown of righteousness...." (2 Timothy 4:7)

We are also running our life's marathon right now; what will we see on our scoreboards?

Fight the good fight of faith!....Be a finisher!!

PRAYER FOR THE WEEK
I pray for every reader of today's post that the Lord will strengthen and equip you to complete your life's race. You will run and fulfil your purpose. You will not fail, fall or falter. Jesus is cheering you on to victory. Amen

Yetty Iriah
Monday Morning Coffee Copyright 2020
Photo: James Weston Copyright123RF.com

Reflective Notes

What have you learnt today?

What changes will you make this week?

Week 18

<u>NO FREE BENEFITS!</u>

Happy Monday people!

I met a young man who had started what his family thought was his dream job, and after his first day at work he told his parents the job was boring! I bet most of you know several young people who have also changed jobs in quick succession for similar reasons.

Today I am concerned that we are raising a generation of young people who want the dream house and dream car but are not prepared to put the work in. These are young people who want the prize but not the process; who want success without commitment.

However, before we point our fingers at them, perhaps we should all take a good look in the mirror too, because the apple does not fall far from the tree. Perhaps we are the generation that is so preoccupied with our selfish desires that we can't mentor, teach or nurture the young people around us, and yet we expect them to succeed.

If you want greatness, you must be prepared to pay the cost! ....There are no free benefits!

PRAYER FOR THE WEEK
I confess that I have been selfish with my time and talent and have hoarded the gifts and wisdom you have blessed me with. Lord, lead me to mentor young people in my family or neighbourhood.

Yetty Iriah
Monday Morning Coffee Copyright 2020
Photo:RawpixelCopyright123RF.com

Reflective Notes

What have you learnt today?

What changes will you make this week?

Week 19

NAME YOUR HURRICANE

Happy Monday people!

According to the United States Met Office, storms alternated between male and female names to make them easier to follow on TV and social media platforms.

This morning let's remember Jonah; the only man who was swallowed by a fish and lived to tell the tale! Jonah was running away from God; as a matter of fact, he was running in the opposite direction, so God sent a storm to hunt him down! I'll like to name the storm 'Hurricane Jonah'! God caused Jonah to be swallowed by a big fish that after three days and three nights vomited him onto the shores of Nineveh; exactly where he was meant to be!....God must have laughed!

"Jonah prayed to the Lord his God from inside the fish. Then the Lord ordered the fish to vomit Jonah onto the dry land." (Jonah 2: 1-10)

I have also encountered several storms in my life in times of disobedience. Often God sends the storms to us get our attention and lead us to a place of repentance.

Perhaps that storm raging in your life now is a hurricane with your own name on it!....Go back to GOD!

ACTION FOR THE WEEK.
This week I want you to reflect on the storms in your life; could God be asking you to make some changes?

Yetty Iriah
Monday Morning Coffee Copyright 2020
Photo:Pixabay.com

Reflective Notes

What have you learnt today?

What changes will you make this week?

Week 20

SMALL IS ENOUGH!

Happy Monday people!

Isn't it strange that the key to our miracle is often hidden in plain sight; in the small stuff, the things we take for granted?

After a major victory on Mount Carmel, Elijah expected to find God in the fire and the earthquake, but God came in a still small voice.

A certain widow's sons were to be sold off to pay a debt their father who had been a prophet owed. (How a prophet died without financial provision for his family is a story for another day!) This widow had a combination of small stuff; a small jar of oil, good neighbours and some empty vessels. This combination turned her into a wealthy oil merchant! **(2 Kings 4: 1-7)**

It was also a small boy's lunch that fed the multitude, with several baskets of left-overs. Look at the small stuff around you too; you may need them one day. **(Matthew 14: 13-21)**

....You only need mustard-seed faith to move huge mountains!

PRAYER FOR THE WEEK
Lord, throughout this week, help me see you in the things and people that I take for granted. Lord, may I never despise the little I have because You are always in it.

Yetty Iriah
Monday Morning Coffee Copyright 2020
Photo: Georges Tsartsianidis Copyright123RF.com

Reflective Notes

What have you learnt today?

What changes will you make this week?

Week 21

DISTINCTLY UNIQUE

Happy Monday people!

As a mother of now 19-year-old twin girls, I nostalgically remember the early years when I dressed them up identically. I had an obsession to make them look exactly the same.... And oh, how they hated it!

On their tenth birthday they announced they will not be wearing identical clothing anymore. I was heartbroken then, but I have now come to terms with the fact that they are two distinctly unique individuals. Today, Emmanuella and Daniella are strong independent young ladies; one an extrovert and the other an introvert, but we celebrate their uniqueness every day. I still miss seeing them in their cute identical outfits and all the attention and lovely comments we always got.... (I got!).

Israel also wanted to be exactly like the other nations and demanded for their own king. God let them have their way, but with catalogue of disastrous consequences. **(1 Samuel 8)**

Today most people strive to be a replica of someone else, yet God has made us all fearfully and wonderfully unique. **(Psalm 139:14)**

<u>Don't be a fake copy of an original!</u>
<u>You are a star too! …. Shine where you are!</u>

PRAYER FOR THE WEEK
Lord I am uniquely made in your exact image and likeness. May I shine for you in all I do this week.

Yetty Iriah
Monday Morning Coffee Copyright 2020
Photo: PhotoroadCopyright123RF.com

Reflective Notes

What have you learnt today?

What changes will you make this week?

Week 22

SHOES OFF!.... PLEASE!

Happy Monday people!

Do you take offence when you visit friends or family, and are asked to take your shoes off at the door? Do you outwardly complain, or grudgingly comply?

Shoes are not just a fashion accessory in the literal sense; they represent who we are, our social standing and background. Our shoes say everything about us. Personally, I pay more attention to my shoes than any other aspect of my dressing.

The burning bush must have been quite a spectacle to behold, but Moses had to take his shoes off before he could approach the miraculous. **(Exodus 3: 1-6)**

"The Lord opposes the proud but gives grace to the humble."
(James 4:6)

Today we approach the Lord in our designer shoes; expecting preferential treatment, while some of us walk in carelessly with dirty shoes and muddy boots, with total disregard for His sacred presence!

If you want to experience the miraculous, you must take your shoes too!
....Even if they are Jimmy Choos or Loubs!

PRAYER FOR THE WEEK
Lord, please forgive me for approaching your presence without respect. Teach me humility so that I may also walk in the miraculous.

Yetty Iriah
Monday Morning Coffee Copyright 2020
Photo:Pixabay.com

Reflective Notes

What have you learnt today?
_____
_____
_____
_____
_____
_____
_____
_____
_____
_____

What changes will you make this week?
_____
_____
_____
_____
_____
_____
_____
_____
_____
_____

Week 23

BUSY BEES!

Happy Monday People!

Have you ever been so busy that you feel rushed off your feet like you're losing your centre of gravity? By nature, I am a very restless woman, I often have my hands in several pies at any one time, and I have to consciously remind myself to take a break!

Life can be a treadmill of activities, and in the midst of this 'legitimate busyness' it is so easy to lose track of where God is and relegate Him to the background. As we rush around, we can so easily miss the glimpses of God around us and the gentle nudging of the Holy Spirit.

Will you be a Martha; so busy serving tables that you forget to eat yourself? Or will you be a Mary; just content to sit at the Master's feet and enjoy sweet fellowship? **(Luke 10:38-42)**

There are several Christians who are so busy with church activities and yet have no relationship with God.

....If we are legitimately too busy for God, then we are too busy wasting time!

PRAYER FOR THE WEEK
Lord, I surrender my time to you, help me reorder my priorities. May I be reminded that any time away from You is wasted time.

Yetty Iriah
Monday Morning Coffee Copyright 2020
Photo: Happetr Copyright 123RF.com

Reflective Notes

What have you learnt today?

What changes will you make this week?

Week 24

WHO NEEDS A MONUMENT?

Happy Monday people!

If you take a trip into Central London, you will be amazed at the number of high-rise office buildings and sky-scrappers. A concrete jungle has emerged overnight just like downtown New York

As the disciples marched into Jerusalem they marvelled at the huge marble-pillared temples and historical monuments, surrounded by carefully laid cobblestone paths. Instantly! Jesus warned them that a day will come when these buildings will all be destroyed! **(Matthew 13:1-13)**

What legacy are we passing to the next generation? Will we build a monument or plant a tree? The Word of God is like a tree; if we teach our children the Word, then we lay down deep roots for generations to come.

"And there arose a generation that did not know the Lord ...."(Judges 2:10)

Sadly, today all over the world most of the monumental cathedrals are empty, some have been converted into luxury hotels or even night clubs!

**Today we have a dotted skyline and a generation without the Word!
The Lord's heart bleeds!....Ours should too!**

PRAYER FOR THE WEEK
Lord I confess that I have totally missed it! I have set any heart on material things in place of Your Word that endures. Grant me the wisdom and power to pass on the legacy of salvation.

Yetty Iriah
Monday Morning Coffee Copyright 2020
Photo:Pixabay.com

Reflective Notes

What have you learnt today?

What changes will you make this week?

Week 25

ALL THAT DRAMA!

Happy Monday people!

My children call me a drama queen, but I always remind them that life would be so boring without a little drama now and again!

Anyone who has read the bible will agree that God also has a penchant for the dramatic. God just loves an audience: I call Him the "show-off" God!

Now as if the burning bush and ten plagues in Egypt were not dramatic enough, God ensured that after centuries in bondage, His chosen people left Egypt in manner of epic proportions, through the Red Sea, defying all logic and drowning all their enemies in one fell swoop!....It must have made headline news! **(Exodus 13: 17-22)**

We all like shortcuts, but if God allowed shortcuts all the time, we will take the credit for our achievements, so instead He takes us the long, hard and windy way so He can put up a show!

*"But I will harden Pharaoh's heart so that I may multiply My signs and My wonders
in the land of Egypt." (Exodus 7:3)*

God will take us through the Red Sea rather than around it, so that He can drown the enemies that are chasing us.

Are you faced with a Red Sea situation?
The show has just begun!....We are all watching!

PRAYER FOR THE WEEK
O Lord, place me in a strategic position both physically and spiritually to see you perform Your signs and wonders in my life this week.

Yetty Iriah
Monday Morning Coffee Copyright 2020
Photo:Elenashow Copyright 123RF.com

Reflective Notes

What have you learnt today?
_____
_____
_____
_____
_____
_____
_____
_____
_____
_____

What changes will you make this week?
_____
_____
_____
_____
_____
_____
_____
_____
_____
_____

Week 26

THIS IS WAR!

Happy Monday people!

Baptist minister Alice McDermott, was a former RAF pilot who had flown several missions into Iraq and Afghanistan, and as I listened to her narrate her first-hand experience of warfare at one of our church conferences, I was amazed at the level of training and preparedness that she had to undergo before her often deadly missions.

I began to draw a parallel with the Christian's level of preparedness in the area of spiritual warfare. Sadly, I fear most of us are open targets for the enemy, because we have no idea we are at war! Our warfare is against unseen wicked forces, but the battle is very real!

*"Therefore put on the full armour of God, so that when the day of evil comes,
you may be able to stand your ground...." (Ephesians 6:13)*

Jesus is our commander-in-chief and we must put on our full armour and await our marching orders!

This is war Friends!
....Are we battle-ready to fly into that storm?

PRAYER FOR THE WEEK
Lord, may I never become a casualty of this invisible war. Clothe me with your armour and give me victory on every side.

Yetty Iriah
Monday Morning Coffee Copyright 2020
Photo: Pixabay.com

Reflective Notes

What have you learnt today?

What changes will you make this week?

Week 27

LET'S GO!

Happy Monday people!

Anyone who has ever driven with me will definitely understand why I had to sit my driving test six times! My husband always has his heart is in his mouth and holds on to his seat for dear life when I am at the wheel!

Now life is never a nice smooth freeway, but a one-way road with several traffic stops, speed bumps, potholes and road blocks....And don't ever forget those sneaky speed cameras!

While we drive facing forward now and again, we need to use our rear-view mirrors to remind ourselves of where we are coming from and how far God has brought us.

Sadly, there are some who live life in reverse, transfixed on the past, unable to make progress and headed for a certain crash!

"Forgetting those things which are behind I press toward the mark for the prize of the high calling of God." (Phillipians 3:13-14)

With God in the driving seat we can trust Him for better days ahead.

Hey! Don't look back!...Remember Lot's wife!

PRAYER FOR THE WEEK
Lord I invite you into the driving seat of my life. Take me as far as you wish me to go. Keep my eye focused on my goal and destination and may I always be reminded of how far you have brought me.

Yetty Iriah
Monday Morning Coffee Copyright 2020
Photo: Oksana Alekseevac Copyright 123RF.com

Reflective Notes

What have you learnt today?
_____
_____
_____
_____
_____
_____
_____
_____
_____
_____

What changes will you make this week?
_____
_____
_____
_____
_____
_____
_____
_____
_____
_____

Week 28

A SUDDEN BREAKTHROUGH!

Happy Monday people!

My post today is inspired by events in the life of one of the most ambitious and restless young men I know.

On what was a normal 'boring' day, Tizzy took a train to meet up with friends in the City of London. Tizzy sat next to a man with a huge rucksack, the mixing deck bulging out from the bag caught his attention and a conversation started. Now this total stranger also took an unusual interest in Tizzy and things just seemed to snowball out of control from then on. Three weeks later Tizzy was hosting his very own show on one of London's foremost radio stations!

Now Ruth the Moabite also left home on a normal morning in search of food, and just 'happened' to step into the field belonging to Boaz.....We know the rest of the story! **(Ruth 2:3)**

Opportunities abound all around, so embrace this mundane Monday morning with renewed zeal and expectation; open your eyes and ears.

The breakthrough you seek is not too far away! ....Perhaps even on a crowded, smelly London Underground train!

PRAYER FOR THE WEEK
I pray that all who will read this post today will meet with extraordinary favour. Great doors will open for you and the Lord will put divine enablers in your life to propel you to your next level.

Yetty Iriah
Monday Morning Coffee Copyright 2020
Photo: Christos Georghiou Copyright123RF.com

Reflective Notes

What have you learnt today?

What changes will you make this week?

Week 29

SHHH!....ZIP IT!

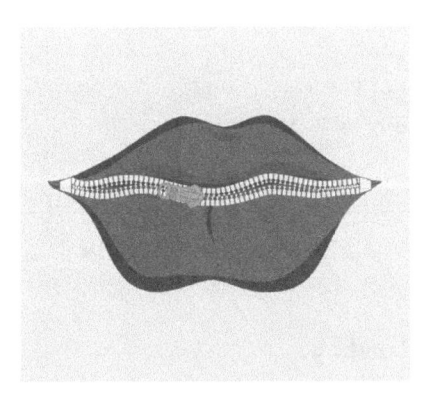

Happy Monday people!

Has your mouth ever put you into trouble? They say the tongue is the smallest organ in the body, but a most dangerous weapon and almost impossible to control.

How does bad language, gossip, slander and lying manage to subtly creep in when we are in so-called good company? Why do the bad words just seem to fly out of our mouths with such reckless abandon like a burst water-pipe?

Have you in the heat of anger hit the 'send' button for that text or email without thinking about how it may be received on the other end? I am one person who is very guilty of this!

They say words once spoken are like dropped eggs that can never be put back together. Whatever is true, whatever is kind and whatever is necessary; that is the Litmus test! **(Philippians 4:8)**

"Death and life are in the power of the tongue, and those who love it will eat its fruits."
(Proverbs 18:21)

Oh, how I shudder at the very thought that we will all give account to God for every idle word spoken!

Now zip those lips quick!....Before they kill you!

PRAYER FOR THE WEEK
Lord, forgive me for the times I have used my mouth to bring down others and say hurtful things. Forgive me for the lack of self-control I exhibit time and time again. Put a watch over my lips and let mouth be filled with praise alone.

Yetty Iriah
Monday Morning Coffee Copyright 2020
Photo: Yupiramos Copyright 123RF.com

Reflective Notes

What have you learnt today?

What changes will you make this week?

Week 30

HARD PRESSED?

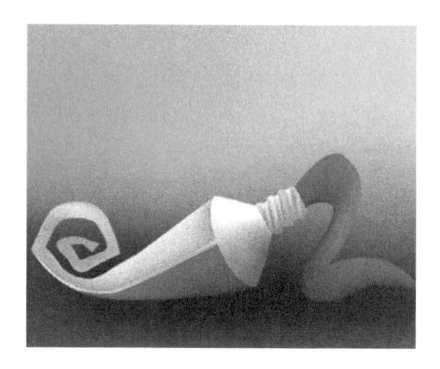

Happy Monday people!

My short piece today is about the toothpaste; some- thing I hope we will all be using this morning!

Have you ever felt that situations and circumstances are choking the life out of you? Always remember that our life's purpose is often revealed during times of severe testing.

> *Paul said, "We are hard pressed on every side, but not crushed;...persecuted, but not abandoned....that the life of Jesus may be revealed in us." (2 Corinthians 4:8-10)*

Until the tube of toothpaste is pressed, there will be no paste, and when the tube is almost empty, we will often squeeze and roll it up from the bottom to the top to get the very last drop out! In the same way God uses our challenges to push us to the limit until every last drop of virtue is poured out.

Don't be like the full tube of toothpaste sitting pretty on the bathroom shelf, of no use to anyone!

If you intend to make a difference, and impact your world, then get ready to be pressed!
....And very hard too!

PRAYER FOR THE WEEK
Lord, may those challenges that seem to push me to the limit mature me and teach me to trust in your unfailing word.

Yetty Iriah
Monday Morning Coffee Copyright 2020
Photo: Aliaksei Papou Copyright 123RF.com

Reflective Notes

What have you learnt today?

What changes will you make this week?

Week 31

THE MASTERS BUSINESS

Happy Monday people!

This morning I am serving your coffee with a huge dose of soul-stirring truths!

The bible tells us that in the last days there will be a lot of buying and selling going on with most people totally oblivious of the times that they are living in.

Life is a marketplace and I will liken it to the typical African market setting where people come from neighbouring towns to buy and sell their produce. We are all in the market right now doing our business. When the market closes then buyers will go home with their goods, and sellers with their money. Sadly, there will be a few individuals who just drifted in, idle observers with nothing to show for all the time spent in the market, just like the man who buried his talent in the ground!

"He gave one five bags of gold, another two bags, and another one bag, each according to his ability. Then he went on his journey." (Matthew 25:15)

The Lord we serve is profit-conscious and has given us gifts and talents to trade with while on earth. What will you have in your hand when He returns? Will you be a problem-solver or a support system? How many lives will you have impacted?

Hurry! Do the Master's business before the market closes!

PRAYER FOR THE WEEK

Lord, may I not be an idle observer or a drifter in the market of life. May I stand before you with profit in my hand and may my time on earth not be a waste.

Yetty Iriah
Monday Morning Coffee Copyright 2020
Photo:vintagestockphotos.com

Reflective Notes

What have you learnt today?
_____
_____
_____
_____
_____
_____
_____
_____
_____
_____

What changes will you make this week?
_____
_____
_____
_____
_____
_____
_____
_____
_____
_____

Week 32

I CAN SEE YOU!

Happy Monday people!

I trust you all had a great weekend. I am sorry but it's another Monday and we have to do it all over again!

I drove into the City of London one evening and was shocked at the number of CCTV cameras I saw. I felt as if I was on the Big Brother Show. Every single building had one. Someone once said that Britain is one of the most watched societies....And rightly so.

Now the experienced criminals know that every camera has its own blind spot, and all they need to do is to find it. Sadly, most of us also choose to believe we can walk in God's blind spots, and we live our lives oblivious of the 'Big Eye' in the sky!

God has no blind spots! He knows our thoughts afar off and weighs our actions. He listens to every idle word. No veil can hide us from Him.

"You know when I sit and when I rise; you perceive my thoughts from afar." (Psalm 139:2)

One day the CCTV recording of our lives will be replayed. Will we be proud of what we see?

There's a Big Eye in the sky and His name is Jesus ....Smile you're on camera!

PRAYER FOR THE WEEK
Lord, there are so many things that I have done that I am ashamed of! Help me live my life in the consciousness that nothing I do is hidden from you!

Yetty Iriah
Monday Morning Coffee Copyright 2020
Photo: Razvan Ionut Dragomirescu Copyright 123RF.com

Reflective Notes

What have you learnt today?

What changes will you make this week?

Week 33

WHICH DOOR LORD?

Happy Monday People!

It's SALE season again! How do you shop? I absolutely hate fitting rooms so I simply pick the items I like, try them on at home, choose the ones that fit and return the rest to the store....I wish it was that easy to make life's choices.

A certain man Elimelech during a severe famine, chose to leave Bethlehem; the land of bread and relocate with his family to Moab. That choice though logical at the time, lead to a series of tragic consequences. **(Ruth 1:1-5)**

Lot chose the rich luscious green land of Sodom and Gomorrah with tragic results; including a pillar of salt which remains as a monument of disobedience today, as well as the sin of incest leading to the birth of the Moabite nation; perennial enemies of Israel.

Our dearmother Eve also chose to eat that delicious-looking apple and look at us now!!

"There is a way that seems right to a man, but its end is the way of death!" (Proverbs 16:25)

Our choice of spouse, career, employment, neighbourhood, or even our children's schools can have serious implications for the future and should never be taken lightly. Someone once said that the greatest career decision one can make is their choice of spouse. (A story for another day!)

Some choices are irrevocable!....choose wisely!

PRAYER FOR THE WEEK
Lord! Today there are countless options before me. Please grant me the wisdom to make the right choice and close every door that leads to disaster!

Yetty Iriah
Monday Morning Coffee Copyright 2020
Photo:Pixabay.com

Reflective Notes

What have you learnt today?

What changes will you make this week?

Week 34

BUILD!

Happy Monday people!
Another hot mug of coffee served up with some soul-searching reflections!

I have studied the book of Nehemiah a number of times and I choose to describe him as not only a church builder, but also a nation builder.

Nehemiah's mission was to rebuild the wall of Jerusalem, which was in ruins. To accomplish this task, Nehemiah raised an army of equally dedicated builders who amidst intense opposition completed the project in just 52 days!....This was dedication. **(Nehemiah 6:15)**

Today the Church of God is in ruins. It is a house divided against itself and it is rapidly crumbling down! Evangelism is now on the back burner, instead there is infighting and tussle for money, power and leadership....A very sad state of affairs indeed! Most churches have fewer new converts; instead the church is full of 'recycled believers' who are moving from one church to the other.

> "A house is divided against itself, cannot stand."
> (Mark 3:25)

We all have a collective responsibility to build the church, and when we tear each other down we are destroying the God's house!

Be a builder!
.... Jesus is not coming back for a divided church!

ACTION FOR THE WEEK

Think about the ways your actions and those of others may have contributed to a division in your local church. What can you do to rebuild broken bridges? The Lord is counting on you.... Start now!

Yetty Iriah
Monday Morning Coffee Copyright 2020
Photo: Jpegwiz Copyright123RF.com

Reflective Notes

What have you learnt today?

What changes will you make this week?

Week 35

ENJOY THE SCENERY

Happy Monday people!

I dedicate this post to two of my dearest friends; one who has raised her four beautiful daughters on her own, through very dark times, and finally her day of joy has dawned! The other has recently welcomed her prodigal son back home!

Indeed life is a journey of contrasting seasons, while some are on the mountain top, others will be in the valley, some will be celebrating success and sadly others mourning loss.

King Solomon described this succinctly in the Book of Ecclesiastes.

"For everything there is a season, a time for every activity under heaven.
A time to be born and a time to die....A time to cry and a time to laugh...."
(Ecclesiastes 3:2-8)

God never guaranteed us a storm-free life but promised to be the anchor in midst of the storms, so that we may overcome.

We can be confident that after our night of weeping, our morning with dawn with joy!

Life is a train journey....Enjoy the scenery, your train may only going through a tunnel!

PRAYER FOR THE WEEK
Lord, help me to be grateful for this season of my life. I may not understand it now but help me trust that you are in total control of every stage.

Yetty Iriah
Monday Morning Coffee Copyright 2020
Photo:Pixabay.com

Reflective Notes

What have you learnt today?
_____
_____
_____
_____
_____
_____
_____
_____
_____
_____

What changes will you make this week?
_____
_____
_____
_____
_____
_____
_____
_____
_____
_____

Week 36

HUSH!....HUSH!

Happy Monday people!

We live in a noisy world, bombarded by the constant ringing of our phones, pings from emails, text messages, Facebook posts and tweets. Add a busy social life into the mix and you have total chaos!....Just like wearing multiple earphones!

How do we hear the Lord's still small voice amidst this 'noise of the flesh'?

Samuel ran to Eli because he mistook the divine call for the call of the flesh. *(1 Samuel: 3)* Sadly, this is what most of us are doing today. Have you received the call of God and didn't hear it or worse still, ignored it? God will not compete with the noise around us or our busy social lives.

*"I called you so often, but you wouldn't come. I reached out to you, but you paid no attention.
You ignored my advice and rejected the correction I offered."
(Proverbs 1:24)*

Don't wait until life's circumstances cause you to slow down and seek God by force! If you are not intentional in listening out for the voice of God, you may never hear Him.

The call that will change your life may come in a still small voice.....Turn down the noise!

PRAYER FOR THE WEEK
Lord, help me to turn off any noise in my life that prevents me from hearing you clearly. May I never miss what you have to say and give me the strength to obey!

Yetty Iriah
Monday Morning Coffee Copyright 2020
Photo: Scott Betts Copyright 123RF.com

Reflective Notes

What have you learnt today?

What changes will you make this week?

Week 37

REJECTS WANTED!

Happy Monday people!

Imagine standing in the scorching heat, inhaling the most pungent odours and getting your hands bruised and dirty as you dig and shove through mounds of earth in search of discarded glass, plastic and metal.

At this very moment someone out there in the world is making a living from that item you threw into the trash can! What we considered as rubbish has become someone's lifeline.

In the same vein Jesus went in a desperate search for the lost and rejected; the tax collectors, harlots, adulterers, demon-possessed and lepers. He once took a detour on a scorching hot afternoon just to meet the woman at the well; a serial adulteress!

"Assuredly, I say, tax collectors and harlots, will enter the kingdom of God before you." (Matthew 21:31)

The good news is that God will not consider our sordid past to determine our blessed future!

Rejects wanted!....Jesus is hiring!....Sign up now!

PRAYER FOR THE WEEK
Lord! Thank you for loving me when nobody would. You died that horrible death just to give me a new name and a glorious future. Today my story has changed!

Yetty Iriah
Monday Morning Coffee Copyright 2020
Photo: Lightwise Copyright 123RF.com

Reflective Notes

What have you learnt today?

What changes will you make this week?

Week 38

RAIN! RAIN!....Go away!

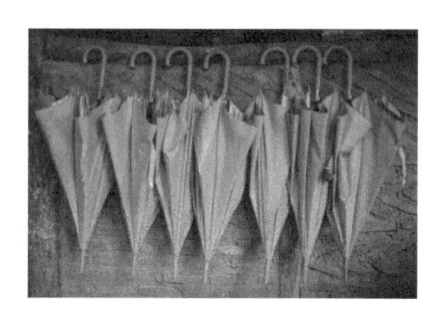

Happy Monday people!

Has an event or series of events ever blown your best laid out plans out of sync? You are not alone.

The Virgin Mary was set to marry Joseph, her childhood sweetheart, I can imagine that wedding invites had been sent out and it was now public knowledge. Suddenly God interrupted the plans and now Mary was to birth a child out of wedlock! Her reputation was at stake; what a disgrace! What would people say? How would she explain this to her family?

God will oftentimes rain on our parade because He wants to parade His own glory. Mary submitted herself to God's will and we should also do the same.

"I am the Lord's servant," Mary answered. "May your word to me be fulfilled." (Luke 1:38)

Sometimes our 'brollies' may need to come out on Parade Day. (Pause for a minute and reflect on this.)

*G*od has no bad weather; even the thunderstorms serve His purpose!....Let it rain Lord!

PRAYER FOR THE WEEK
Lord, You hold the world in Your hands. I submit my plans to you, interrupt them as You see fit in a way that Your name alone is glorified, and help me to be thankful.

Yetty Iriah
Monday Morning Coffee Copyright 2020
Photo: Kuponjabah Copyright 123RF.com

Reflective Notes

What have you learnt today?

What changes will you make this week?

Week 39

THE CHAIN-BREAKER!

Happy Monday people!

My post this morning is dedicated to those in a crisis, and for whom praise does not seem like a viable option now.

Praise is the most powerful weapon to use in the face of a crisis. It breaks every cycle of defeat and discouragement. Praise is a well-known but rarely used weapon of war. It was only praise that brought down the Wall of Jericho.

You may wonder how one is expected to raise hands in praise with a child in the grip of a drug addiction, or a marriage on the brink? How do you praise God with a bad medical report in your hands or when your home is just one step away from repossession?

Two men Paul and Silas raised an altar of praise in the midst their chains, today we can also choose to do the same. **(Acts 16: 25-26)**

Don't hang up your harps yet. You can still sing the Lord's song in a strange land. **(Ps 137)**

Break your chains with your praise! .....Praise works!

ACTION FOR THE WEEK
All this week spend time in deliberate praise to God and see those chains break!....... Please don't forget to share your chain-breaking testimony.

Yetty Iriah
Monday Morning Coffee Copyright 2020
Photo:Pixabay

Reflective Notes

What have you learnt today?

What changes will you make this week?

Week 40

WHICH IS YOUR CROSS?

Happy Monday people!

When life happens, and situations weigh us down, we have a tendency to complain about the weight of our cross or compare ourselves with those who carry seemingly lighter crosses. Do you agree?

Simon of Cyrene, a Gentile convert was passing through Jerusalem, when he came upon the unfolding bloody spectacle; bleeding Jesus buckling under the weight of His heavy cross. Suddenly! Simon was seized from the crowd and forced to carry the heavy cross uphill behind Jesus. Simon just happened to be in the crowd on that day, going about his own business. The heavy cross was forced on him; he did not have a choice! **(Luke 23:26)**

"The temptations in your life are no different from what others experience, but God is faithful, He will not allow the temptation to be more than you can stand. "
(1 Corinthians 10:13)

The crosses we bear in life are not of our own choosing, and we may want to swap crosses if we had a chance. Just like Simon, our crosses are just thrust on us suddenly; often without warning!

Sorry dear! You can't choose your own cross!

PRAYER FOR THE WEEK
O Lord! The cross I carry feels so heavy, but you always provide the strength to bear it. Forgive me for grumbling and as I follow Jesus may I find purpose in my pain.

Yetty Iriah
Monday Morning Coffee Copyright 2020
Photo: Pixabay

Reflective Notes

What have you learnt today?

What changes will you make this week?

Week 41

ATTENTION!....FRUIT LOVERS!

Happy Monday people!

Have you had your 5 a day this morning? Don't you just love this "star studded" fruit selection? ....Yummy!

I enjoy eating most fruits, but I can be quite lazy about having to cut, peel or core certain fruits. It's so easy for me to grab a banana or an apple to munch on my drive to work, but that sweet pineapple with its thorny skin and prickly crown may just sit in my fruit basket for a very long time. It's easier just to buy the ready- diced selection from the supermarket.

This morning let's consider another kind of fruit; the Fruit of the Spirit...

"For the Fruits of the Spirit are love, joy, peace, patience, kindness, goodness, faithfulness, gentleness and self-control."
(Galatians 5:22-23)

Now we can't be picky with the fruit of the Spirit. We can't choose joy but then refuse to be patient and kind. We can't opt for peace but refuse to be gentle, and there is no readymade supermarket selection.

Now what's missing in your fruit basket?....Self-control? Patience?

The Fruits of the Spirit are not optional.

PRAYER FOR THE WEEK
Father, help me develop the spiritual fruit that I am missing (name them), so that I may measure up to the nature and character of your son Jesus Christ.

Yetty Iriah
Monday Morning Coffee Copyright 2020
Photo: Nitr Copyright 123RF.com

Reflective Notes

What have you learnt today?

What changes will you make this week?

Week 42

THE EMPTY WAITING ROOM

Happy Monday people!

Waiting is one of the most challenging things we have to endure as Christians. I once heard a preacher describe God as "Jehovah Slow"! I definitely agree that from a human stand-point it is so easy to feel that God is slow to act and to be honest, often He sure takes His time, yet the only choice we have is to wait.

> *"I wait for the Lord, my soul waits, and in His word I do hope. My soul waits for the Lord more than those who watch for the morning—Yes, more than those who watch for the morning." (Psalm 130:5-6)*

Anna and Simeon were two individuals who spent their lifetime waiting for the birth of the promised Messiah. They waited in hope for many years, never giving up hope and in the end they both saw Him! **(Luke 2:25-38)**

Today waiting rooms all over the world are empty! Have you given up too?

Faith is a waiting game!....God never comes late for those who wait.

PRAYER FOR THE WEEK
Lord, please forgive me for leaving the waiting room so prematurely! Forgive me for not trusting you to fulfil your promises concerning my situation. Today I return back to the waiting room confident that you will come through for me.

Yetty Iriah
Monday Morning Coffee Copyright 2020
Photo: Paolo De Santis Copyright 123RF.com

Reflective Notes

What have you learnt today?

What changes will you make this week?

Week 43

CALL THE DOCTOR!

Happy Monday people!

This morning I am serving your morning coffee with a cocktail of pills. There are the sugar-coated multivitamins, and the bitter nausea- provoking antibiotic capsules you'd wish you didn't have to take, but you know are the most important!

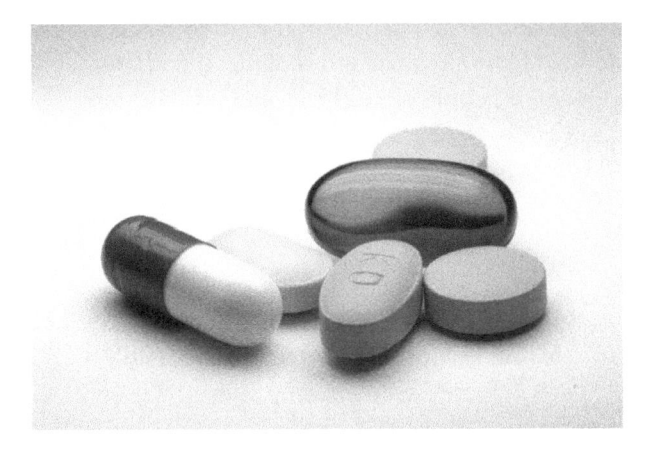

Relationships are like a cocktail of pills, the good, the bad and ugly (nasty). That condescending boss, the domineering husband or nagging wife, unruly teenagers, obnoxious in-laws, and those two-faced friends; the lovely people the Lord put in our lives for a time and season to teach us patience.... Oh! That magic word!

Apostle Paul spoke of a thorn in his flesh; could that have been a toxic relationship?

" A thorn in the flesh was given to me....I asked the Lord three times that it would depart from me. But He said to me, "My grace is enough for you" (2 Corinthians 12:7-9)

How do you deal with those relationships that test your patience to the limit?

Some relationships are like bitter pills, but if you want to get better, you must swallow them!

PRAYER FOR THE WEEK
Lord, You have put certain people in my life to teach me patience. Help me to love the unlovable and radiate your character and nature even when people are difficult and unreasonable.

Yetty Iriah
Monday Morning Coffee Copyright 2020
Photo:Pixabay.com

Reflective Notes

What have you learnt today?
_____
_____
_____
_____
_____
_____
_____
_____
_____
_____

What changes will you make this week?
_____
_____
_____
_____
_____
_____
_____
_____
_____
_____

Week 44

DIVIDED LOYALTY

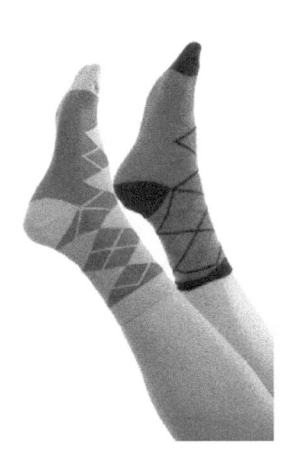

Happy Monday people!
In my part of the world, it's the beginning of autumn, my favourite season; the season for socks and boots. Oh! how I love my boots.

Now on the issue of socks, almost every parent will be used to seeing their teenagers with odd socks on. I used to fuss about this in my household until I realised that no teenager wanted to spend precious time in the laundry basket searching for matching socks.

Now I wonder how God feels when He sees us with odd socks on. We look like people with one foot in the church and the other in the world, trying to eat our cake and have it at the same time, loving

God and loving the world. We all know that with God there is no room for compromise.

> *"No man can serve two masters: for he will either hate one, and love the other...." (Matthew 6:24)*

In what ways are you trying to serve two masters? You can't be a Republican and a Democrat at the same time. Where does your loyalty lie? If you are a Christian, then show it. In what areas of your life are you still sitting on the fence?

**"Let's end the compromise!
....Eternity has no middle ground."**

PRAYER FOR THE WEEK
Lord, deliver me and my household from the spirit of compromise. May we serve you with wholehearted commitment.

**Yetty Iriah
Monday Morning Coffee Copyright 2020**
Photo: Vince Clements Copyright 123RF.com

Reflective Notes

What have you learnt today?
_____
_____
_____
_____
_____
_____
_____
_____
_____
_____

What changes will you make this week?
_____
_____
_____
_____
_____
_____
_____
_____
_____
_____

Week 45

THE HALL OF FAME

Happy Monday People!

Our women's group met one Saturday for an evening hang-out and we each nominated our bible heroines. Great women like Esther, Deborah, Ruth and Hannah topped the list, but interestingly no one chose the woman that was caught in adultery. I believe we should all identify with this nameless woman, because just like her we have received the grace of forgiveness and sanctification.

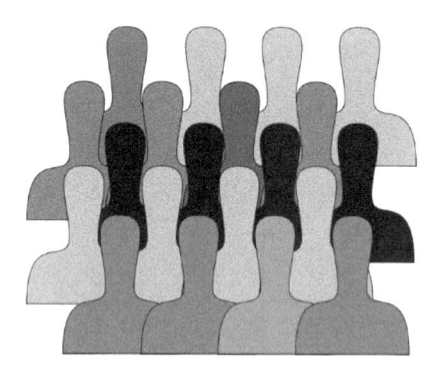

How about the nameless woman at the well of Sychar; the lovely lady who was on her sixth husband? After that divine encounter with Jesus she became a brand new vessel in His hands!
(John 4:1-42)

Next is Jochebed, a mother who against all odds determined that baby Moses will not fall victim to the evil decree of Pharaoh. Every family needs a Jochebed, a woman who will boldly declare "Not on my watch!" Will you be that woman? **(Exodus 2:2)**

Of course, how could we forget Jezebel, Lot's wife and Sapphira? We concluded that in all honesty there are traits of these three women even in the best of us!....Don't you agree?

If the Bible was written again, will you make the headlines? What would be said about you?

PRAYER FOR THE WEEK
For readers of today's post, I pray you will be an individual who will impact your world, and your name will count for God and the gospel for generations to come.

Yetty Iriah
Monday Morning Coffee Copyright 2020
Photo:Pixabay

Reflective Notes

What have you learnt today?

What changes will you make this week?

Week 46

FOR THE FASHIONISTA

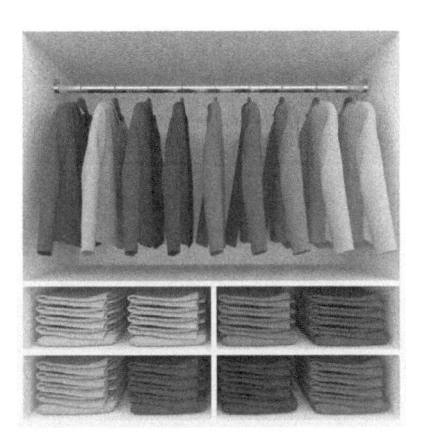

Happy Monday people!

Have you shopped in your wardrobe lately? Or are you one of those who buy a new outfit for every occasion?

We should all have some timeless pieces in our wardrobes, like the little black dress or the white shirt that goes with everything.

In the things of the Spirit also there are some timeless pieces of clothing that must be in every wardrobe.

> *"....Clothe yourselves with compassion, kindness, humility, gentleness and patience, forgive one another ....Above all put on love."*
> *(Colossians 3:12-14)*

In this world where appearance means everything, we must ensure that we adorn our insides just as much as we focus on our outward appearance. People may forget the gifts we give them, but they will never forget how we make them feel. Remember, even Jezebel was a very beautiful woman!

What will you wear today?

<u>A real fashionista always wears love!</u>
<u>....It goes with everything!</u>

PRAYER FOR THE WEEK
Lord! Help me put on love that will radiate from the inside out and this week may people be drawn to You through the love that I show them.

Yetty Iriah
Monday Morning Coffee Copyright 2020
Photo: Suwatchai Pluemruetai Copyright 123RF.com

Reflective Notes

What have you learnt today?

What changes will you make this week?

Week 47

....THAT SMELLS SO GOOD!

Happy Monday people!

We all have that one expensive perfume we only use for special occasions. Mine is Le Gemme by Bvlgari; it was a Christmas present from my son. I call it my Alabaster box!

One woman knelt before Jesus and broke her own Alabaster box, pouring its costly contents onto His feet. Everyone in the room looked at her and wondered why she would waste such an expensive fragrance....But this woman knew why!

**Jesus said, "....Therefore I tell you, her sins, which are many, are forgiven, for she loved much.
But he who is forgiven little, loves little."**
(Luke 7:36-50)

Cece Winans sang a song....

"Don't be angry if I wash His feet with my tears."
"You weren't there the night He found me....."
"And you don't know the cost of the oil in my alabaster box."

What can't we give to the One who freely gave us everything? Until our Alabaster box is broken, there will be no fragrance!

Break your Alabaster box and let the Lord smell something nice!
....Because you know why!

ACTION FOR THE WEEK
Listen to the song "The Alabaster Box" by Cece Winans and give God the fragrance He deserves.

Yetty Iriah
Monday Morning Coffee Copyright 2020
Photo:Vaclav Volrab Copyright 123RF.com

Reflective Notes

What have you learnt today?
_____
_____
_____
_____
_____
_____
_____
_____
_____
_____

What changes will you make this week?
_____
_____
_____
_____
_____
_____
_____
_____

Week 48

THE DREAM TEAM

Happy Monday people!

Don't be surprised that not everyone will support your dream? Interestingly, the people closest to you are most likely to either discourage you or even actively oppose you.

I once watched basketball player Paul Pierce get his No.34 jersey retired by the Boston Celtics. Paul paid an extremely emotional tribute to his mother, who singlehandedly raised him and four brothers in the deprived crime-ridden neighbourhood of Oakland, California.

Among the many tributes, Paul did not forget an uncle who had erected a makeshift basketball hoop in his backyard when it became too dangerous to go out for practice; this was where his basketball dream was birthed!

Paul said "People see the finished product, but not the behind-the-scenes journey or those who influenced it."

Today spare a thought for those who have impacted your life, including those who put the obstacles in your way and inadvertently pushed you in the direction of your dreams; they all make up your dream team.

You could be a part of someone's success story too!
....Don't be a dream killer!

ACTION FOR THE WEEK
This morning as you sip your coffee, write down a list of all your influencers, then make a daily commitment to pray for everyone on that list. This is your Dream Team!

Yetty Iriah
Monday Morning Coffee Copyright 2020
Photo:Pixabay.com

Reflective Notes

What have you learnt today?

What changes will you make this week?

Week 49

THE SOIL OF UNCERTAINTY

Happy Monday people!
This week's post is for those who feel the year is coming to a close and yet believe they are way behind schedule.

When a farmer plants his seed, he does not stay awake all night watching to see the crop grow; neither does he uproot the seed after a few days to see what is happening to it. The real test of faith is when the seed is in the soil and this is where most people miss it!

How do you keep believing for what you can't see? How do you hope against hope? This was Joseph's lot, when he was abandoned in the dungeon of the prison for several years until the day he was summoned by Pharaoh.

"Pharaoh sent and called Joseph, and they brought him quickly out of the dungeon;
he shaved, changed his clothing, and stood before Pharaoh"
(Genesis 41:14)

While Joseph was in prison God was working underground, setting in motion a chain of events that not only led to his release, but also to his promotion. Don't let your dreams die in the soil, God is working underground for you too!

Something is growing in the soil for you!
....And it's very pretty!

PRAYER FOR THE WEEK
Lord! What great comfort to know that while I may be feeling discouraged and abandoned, you are working underground to set me up for victory! Please give the grace to wait.

Yetty Iriah
Monday Morning Coffee Copyright 2020
Photo: Andre Kuzmin Copyright 123RF.com

Reflective Notes

What have you learnt today?

What changes will you make this week?

Week 50

FAITH ON A TIGHTROPE

Happy Monday people!

One of my favourite movies is 'The Walk' a biographical drama based on the true story of Philippe Petit's walk on a tightrope between the Twin Towers of the World Trade Centre. This is one movie that will definitely keep you at the edge of your seat!

God will often take us through the valley the shadow of death to test our faith; sadly, most of us fail here!

It's so easy to trust God for our finances when we still have a good balance on our credit card, and it's easy trust God for healing when faced with an illness we know is not terminal.

Abraham was prepared to kill Isaac; the three Hebrew boys were prepared to be roasted in fire and Daniel was ready to be mauled by the hungry lions. Esther was also prepared to perish if it came to it.

"When you go through deep waters, I will be with you. When you go through rivers of difficulty, you will not drown. When you walk through the fire of oppression, you will not be burnt...."
(Isaiah 43:2)

Do we have the courage to step out in faith and join Jesus on the tightrope too?

Fret not! You are safe and secure in the hands of the One who carries you!

PRAYER FOR THE WEEK
Lord give me the grace to trust you completely even when my faith is on the wire.

Yetty Iriah
Monday Morning Coffee Copyright 2020
Photo: Henry Nine Copyright 123RF.com

Reflective Notes

What have you learnt today?

What changes will you make this week?

Week 51

BRING YOUR GIFTS

Happy Monday people!

It's Christmas again; that frenzied expensive season! In our mad rush to get things ready we must intentionally remind ourselves of the essence of the season, while at the same time keep an eye on our spending.

The three wise men from the East came to see Baby Jesus, bearing their own precious gifts. **(Matthew 2:1)**

Is there a present for Jesus under your Christmas tree too? What will you give Him this year? The Lord is not expecting a gift of silver or gold. He only wants a contrite heart, renewed commitment and reconciliation.

"The sacrifice you desire is a broken spirit. You will not reject a broken and repentant heart."
(Psalm 51:17)

The Lord wants a changed life!....Let's make that our gift to Him this Christmas and share his love with others!

There's no perfect Christmas without Christ!

MERRY CHRISTMAS EVERYONE!

ACTION FOR THE WEEK
If you were giving Jesus a gift today what 3 things will you bring him?

Yetty Iriah
Monday Morning Coffee Copyright 2020
Photo:Pixabay

Reflective Notes

What have you learnt today?

What changes will you make this week?

Week 52

NEW LIFE!...HERE I COME!

Happy Monday people!

This is the last week of the year. For most it will be a week of reflection, setting new goals and making resolutions; which we all know are often never kept! This should be a foundation laying week for the New Year, and we need to get it right.

> *"No one puts new wine into old wineskins; or the new wine will burst the wineskins, new wine must be put into new wineskins, so both are preserved."*
> **(Luke 5:37-38)**

Old wineskins may represent a variety of things; old habits, old relationships, old mind-sets, or even an old location. We tend to hold on to the old because of familiarity and fear of the unknown, or fear of what people may say. Some of us may need to shut an old door and walk away without looking back, lest we turn into a pillar of salt like Lot's wife!

As you make plans for the New Year, do yourself a favour; get rid of those old wineskins!

Remember, New Year, New Goals, New Life....New You!

PRAYER FOR THE WEEK
O Lord, give me the boldness to shut doors that need to be shut and walk away without looking back at what is already lost. Show me a glimpse of my promised future.

Yetty Iriah
Monday Morning Coffee Copyright 2020
Photo: Costasz Copyright 123RF.com

Reflective Notes

What have you learnt today?

What changes will you make this week?

SING A NEW SONG

.... Your Bonus Cup of Coffee

Happy Monday People!
This is an extra cup of my delicious coffee served with a large dose of HOPE!

I once listened to an intensely emotional testimony of a man delivered from a 20 year bout of severe pain and 10 year battle with a psychotic illness, alcoholism and drug addiction....The perfect 'miry clay' combination!

Nothing describes a place of darkness, despair and uncertainty as vividly as the miry clay. In the miry clay one is going on a downward spiral and knows it. It is a bottomless pit of quicksand and the more you move the more you sink!

King David described his own encounter with God in the miry clay:

"I waited patiently for the LORD to help me, and he heard my cry. He lifted me out of the pit of despair and set my feet on solid ground. He has given me a new song to sing; many will see what He has done and be amazed. They will put their trust in the LORD." **(Psalm 40:1-3)**

Today this man's new song is drawing others to place their trust in God!

....You will be singing your new song next!

Yetty Iriah
Monday Morning Coffee Copyright 2020
Photo: Pixabay.com

Reflective Notes

What have you learnt today?
_____
_____
_____
_____
_____
_____
_____
_____
_____

What changes will you make this week?
_____
_____
_____
_____
_____
_____
_____
_____
_____

BOOK REVIEW

Monday Morning Coffee is a collection of self-reflective devotionals; it makes the reader look at themselves in the mirror, with reference to the teachings of Jesus Christ and nicely tying it into modern day reference, covering topics on friendship, family, salvation, eternity, forgiveness, devotion to God, the precious nature of time and many more. One of Yetty's many catchy phrases is *"Let's reflect on some soul-stirring truths."*

Monday Morning Coffee reflections are accompanied by very colourful imagery giving out a strong pictorial message. On a personal note, one of my favourites is the devotional titled "Sing A New Song" added as a bonus reflection at the back of this book, where the writer shares an emotional testimony of a man delivered from 20 years of severe pain and a 10 year battle with a psychotic illness, alcoholism and drug addiction. In Yetty's words "The perfect miry clay combination!" What a humbling combination as she goes on to share King David's description of his encounter with God in the miry clay....Very moving!

Yetty Iriah writes with a heart of passion to get the reader closer to God from the inside. This is a most inspiring devotional to read.

NONYELUM IKE-OTUONYE

DIVINE MEMOIRS
September 2019

THANK YOU

It has been an absolute honour to have served you all your steaming-hot cups of delicious 'Monday Morning Coffee' throughout the year.

I have enjoyed every minute journeying this challenging but awesome year with you. We have shared our triumphs and disappointments and have loved and served the Lord together. Thank you for sharing your lives and hearts with me.

I look forward to serving you again in the New Year.

Yetty Iriah ♡
Monday Morning Coffee Copyright 2020
Photo by Tatish designs @123RF